after the fall of a cloud

poems

after the fall of a cloud

poems

Oindri Sengupta

Hawakal
PUBLISHERS
New Delhi | Calcutta

HAWAKAL
New Delhi | Calcutta

HAWAKAL PUBLISHERS
70 B/9 Amritpuri, East of Kailash, New Delhi 65
33/1/2 K B Sarani, Mall Road, Calcutta 80

Email info@hawakal.com
Website www.hawakal.com

Cover photo & designed by Bitan Chakraborty

First edition (paperback) February 2022

ISBN: 978-93-91431-46-4 (paperback)

Price: INR 300 | USD 13.99

for

Ma

whose hands showed me the flowers of the Sun

CONTENTS

FEBRUARIES

Cold winter running down my spine.
Wet night is chilling my senses—
making me crippled as insects under the soil.
Lazy falling of rain drops
in my soul.
I hear.

I am in an asylum—
under treatment.

I sit beside my window
and sleep.
Freud speaks in my dreams,
Plath, in my conscience.
Ashes pile around me
and knocks at statutory warning.
I shut the window.

Pictures of fake reality
stare at my empty faces
and creep in my flesh.

I love writing Yeats on wall,
the white, untainted wall of freedom,
the cool park that I visit at times
and walk among swans,
dipped in sandy waters of time.

Tomorrow was my birthday.
Radio, television, newspaper are busy proclaiming
that fake frenzied madness.
Madness, that is me.
myself.

Rain hasn't stopped yet.

Rose is the Name

Name of the sun is Rose.
One that blooms like a winter
in the corner of my room
and lights up the golden evenings.

Name walks within my bolted fingers
to open a blue space of the nerves.
I ride through the age of salt and pebbles,
through the solitary eyes of the name.

I go back to the hour
where I fermented the soil
with the blood of my womb.

I go back to that hour of disguise
to know that the sun needs a name
to rise above the sky and burn
like a thunder.

I WANT TO BE A WHITE WIND

I want to be a white wind
that blows in winter with the smell
of summer and cilantro.
The cilantro has a taste of night
when it loses its anonymity,
and sleeps no more in the dark
but rides on the grey horses of morning.

I want to be a white wind,
which your eyes carry to me
in the silent hours of your love
when the bird of autumn
digs its nest in the grave.

The wind in your eyes
is too full with the colours of white moon
and it swims in my blood
like a fish in the dead sea.

I want to be a white wind,
that gives me breath in your lips
when the night rises from your waist
and wraps me in its splendor.

A HOME WITHIN

There is a home within a home.
A home where stories of lives give birth
to many others to be left untold.
A place of beautiful wanderings and solitude.
When a crow forgets to return to its nest
because it remembers too much of the light,
the home that lives within, comes alive
with all its fruitless longings.

Our wanderings are always with the moon.
And in this long journey to death
I have come to know that home
is another illusion born out of those moments
when we were busy separating light and darkness.

SEVEN STEPS TO THE SUN

Sun looks grey today.
It fell on my hollowed cheeks like two
ripened apples on a moss covered valley.
I heard that the sun too changes its colours.
All you need is to give your skin
and see how many of them look like yours.

I have seen mine.
Some looked like soldiers in a Long March
walking with a sack of yellow roses,
while some were like a river
building stories around her bank
like the vanishing shadows of flying birds.

Our love for sun is like the thirst-laden paths
stretching over the paradoxes of our existence,
defining our lives with its colours.

LOVE – A DIFFICULTY

Love is another difficulty
that fixes you inside a hollow
like the centre of a supernova,
unsettling all the moments
that were grasping your fingers
from falling over the stubborn days.

When the sun felt lighter on skin and
not like those when your thoughts
tore you apart,
love felt like a dreamer's soliloquy
gliding through the feather of night,
whispering softly what morning flowers
tell the sun about all the whys of springs.

I had the vision of a land where
love would fall from the fading moon
to give birth to another
that comes only when the sky dreams
after the fall of a cloud.
Our vanity is too big to hold all that love.

HOW NOT TO BE

Sometimes all I want to do is just breathe.
After sleeping with a spoonful of stars
under my skin
I forgot those scalded hands
that scooped a day out of those nights.

Sleeping is oblivion's second child.
The fireflies that invade my night
are the droplets of an ocean I saw—
when my eyes wore the blue water of a fig tree
to dissipate the glowing wind.

Sometimes all I want to do is just breathe
the entire sea inside my lungs.

Carry me to the edge of the moon and
I would tell you where
the heart of winter lies.

LIGHT THAT FALLS

It was a time when
I tilled the land with my hands
to see if the scent of soil can speak
of paper birds that you left for me somewhere
inside the glowing embers of night.
Listen! Said the rising dew drops.
And I heard the symphonic wind that
blew inside me was the sound of their wings
flapping like memories on the mountain top.

To hold my darkness,
you should be as light as the moon,
or else I would sink, like the sea.

CROSSING THE LAND

Tonight when stars will rest on the sea shore
from long journey of crossing the shores of death,
I will move from the corals of sand
to the light of darkness,
where my loneliness will be crowned with waters
which I left behind in my wings of memories.

Tonight when the wind will rest in melancholy,
I will travel to a faraway land to sow crops
in the field of passion,
to grow life from the corpse that the sea gave me.

Tonight when all hungers of stone will disappear
from the eyes of sea birds
and the sky will pour into dews of rain,
my pen will march towards the poetry of waves
with which the sea will write for the pains of man.

SOLITUDE IS A SONG

Sometimes solitude tastes
like the numb strumming of a guitar
that falls on a lazy afternoon like
the accidental appearance of a monk,
when you were about to tell yourself
that life is full of iridescent colours of monotony.
And when you sit with a few hours of sand
that suddenly drops from the wings of retreating bird,
solitude shows that life is a number
which has a memory of its own
like a forlorn café at the end of a street,
waiting for its number arrive.
And when you learn to carry it
through the mist of time,
it brings you back the rose you left behind
for all the hundred evolving springs.

Strange Meetings

We meet as strangers—
in the cornered agony of a lifeless river,
among the ticking of clock
and nightly song of crickets.

We meet in the empty sky
of a time forgotten era,
mirroring empty shadow on our crushed bodies,
and castrated emotions.

Reality gives life an illusory reality.
And we move on
towards the morning table
where tea is being laid.

We meet as strangers
in this island of nowhere,
playing merry-go-round
with our masked identities.

Falling Leaves

Looking beyond the silences of night
the figures dance around me,
as the moonlight dances around my naked window.
With their slow, evading footsteps
I hear the falling rains
of the yesteryears' morning song
going arid in my dry brows.

I am watched. And judged—
till my hands are dyed with blood,
and I lie
in this land of dead rivers. Dead suns.
Deadened darkness over my rooftop,
over my barren land
where I crawl to walk.

And here I am at peace.
The peace of the dead.

INTO THE HOLLOW

Like meeting of two waves at the horizon,
the cold days of my summer pass
with the notes of a tambourine.
There I found the leaves of your eyes fall
like a sinking ship with half-written stories.
To know where the last days of a storm lie,
I must stand where the evening builds its home.
But my home is lost when I tried to find one.

Far into the depths of a meandering river,
the wind speaks with the voice of a rock to emancipate
the red riding hoods from becoming a story.
Far into the depths of all the raging fires
grows a fountain of darkness.
Like the smoke rising out of the cup,
where you hold dreams from falling apart,
I see a lighthouse gilding into the desert
and invoking the sea with its fingers.

A VALLEY OF SUNSHINE

In the fingers of my son with which
he shows me rain,
grows a deep valley of sunshine.

I sit with him under the boughs of everyday monotony,
with my hands cluttered with the rust of life,
trying to create days from endless nights.
But then with his colours he comes;
strikes a few lines on the wall,
and I see all the lights and darkness fading in them,
like a vision in rain.
What remains is a glorious vast sky
and a few dots of trees on it.

There is an element of spontaneity in those fingers.
Like water they flow over those walls, over my dreams
and sometimes over my face and hands,
mixing fantasy with reality.
I sit submerged in their movement.

He knows when the moon shines
and when the cloud calls,
when the sky begins to shower, or

which word is missing in my song.
He shows me all,
which I had never known before.

In the fingers of my son,
grows a deep valley of sunshine—
as deep as the heart of the earth.

Intersection

After years of lost journeys
I've found a rose—
over desolate banks, green fields,
where the squirrel brings
a swelling river with its tail.
Like the lotus mornings,
where the moths seldom rise
from the love of their songs,
the rose is born inside me.

When you see the sunset waking up
from its slender shadow,
adorning the grief with its broken fingers,
you should know that I've arrived.

Lost tales are not always found
inside unopened doors.
Those can be heard among the unspoken words of trees,
among all the Byzantium roads
that lead us to each other.
They are like the falling feathers of a sparrow.

No one knows where all of them begin,
and where they end.

INFINITY

It takes years for the light to pass through a shadow.
It takes years for the moon to burn like dew.
Years. Days. Months—
all that ticks inside our fingers,
are the journey of a leaf inside the storm.

When sun travels to the other world,
I become a tree.
My feet grows into soil to find scales of fish.
Through my hands, water flows
like the melancholy of stars.

I live inside multiple spaces at the same time,
swimming from one vernal light, to the light of the fall.
Coming of age stories are not for me.
I teach my arms how to fix an empty lampshade
when the light outside is too blinding.
I rise like the sound of a woodcutter's axe,
deep, airy and full of trepidations.

Voices are colorless shadows,
engulfing us whenever we try to find ourselves.

The Last Mile

Sound of stars carries the silence of universe.
At night when a light drops into river,
a star is born.
The river is nameless.
It has a home where it builds ocean from its droplets.
The star too is nameless.
And its home is where the world ends.

I was once friend to someone whom I knew
before I came to know myself.
I knew her the way each star carries
knowledge of sun inside it,
and the world plants its shadows
on a blooming flower.
I knew her till I remembered to remove
stains from the mirror.

So much has been lost since then.
So less has been said and known.
Now all that fills up my throat is the silence of the sea.
And numbers still remain a mystery for me.

Hundred And One Stories Of Rain

Stories of rain never end
as they have no beginning.
They have no hurry to start
with a few empty alphabets,
staring through the walls around them.
Nor do they have to end like light
where the tunnel curves into another galaxy.

My days were replete with all the stories
that an afternoon rain could bring.
My mother would sit with her open hair,
water dripping slowly down her shoulders
telling me how to see 'Kali' in the dark clouds,
the mother who lives inside us.
She would smell of rain, of the mysterious smell of soil
and the room would turn into a beautiful aroma—
like the one that lingers every time
we wake up from a dream.

I listened and found stars in rain.
I dropped a few along the way to another land.

Stories of rain never end.
They flow like the memories of my smiling mother,
abundant and everlasting like sunshine after a storm.

RESURRECTION

I never wanted to die.
But death is like a letter you write every time
that reaches nowhere because no one existed.
Returning is never easy, and
death comes every day.
It comes every night like a song without break,
like a friend whose doors are never closed.
So I die. And live again.
I live because I never wanted to return
to the land that was never mine.

The house where I was born
died the night my mother left me.
It was dark and the moon was hanging like a corpse.
Since then my hand smells of the colours of water
and of blue sands.
And every time I return here I see her faint blue eyes
looking through the void of a river.

I never wanted to die.
So I turn the leaves of tree to the sun
and turn them back again when it rains.

BIRTH

This is the place where I first arrived,
when I was…
The darkness, shades of coconut trees,
smell of summer rain, the nests of sparrows—
welcomed my little eyes.

I arrived here alone,
lonely as the first rain on mahogany leaves.

Sky used to be younger then,
and had a voice of its own.
It was that voice, which first taught me to sing,
and my loneliness soon turned into a song.

Amid that vastness,
my soul spreads its wings in the wind,
in the soft light of the stars,
towards the maiden light of the sun.

BEGINNING TO BEGIN

To begin is to walk on the earth's edge
and measure its sorrows,
as the light weighs its weight on the earth.
To begin is to know once again that
the thought which brought you here
was once a flower's obsession with wind.

Like a century old song that promises
you of a lost time,
beginning captures our endless journey with the self,
shows us a swan's dilemma on the eyes of water
and a vision to carry its song inside it.

To begin is to hear what ears cannot
and to understand what the forests say
about minds of man.

INSIGNIFICANT WANDERINGS

I've left the sea at the parched door of oblivion
where your eyes stood to receive my empty eyes.
Someone said words have meanings only if we know
how to listen to the sky when a lightning strikes.

To listen is to completely disown yourself
like the leaves at the end of rain.

I have left the sea where the salt has left its scars
over stones and rocks.
I have left it to know how not to begin.

It's been years since I visited her shore
and wrote my name on her.

Sometimes all you need is a sea to fly,
and a little wind in your hair.

SOLITARY EARTH

Earth has lost its balance.
Hundred years of walking over the sea of sands
has built walls in her roots.

Waking is a different dream.
Like time travels under the sea,
earth evokes the splendor of awakening
in the eyes of morning birds.

From the dream that was lost on the shore of sky,
I fail to assume winter fruits in summer's song.
Hence I go plucking from flower to flower,
from one sea to the other
with the hope of raising a home for her
in the field of butterflies.

What we lose today is not always lost.
Somewhere it leaves its tiniest seed
to grow into a river and sun--
to begin where it ended.

In our house

In our house lives a sorrow.
When the rain had last forgotten to arrive,
it came through our western window,
perched on our floor and when we walk,
it gathers as sweat around our toes.

When we were having the coffee of winter
at the backyard of our house,
it was wearing the mask of a forgetful dream,
where we meet ourselves
and sleepwalk through the end of horizon.

It gave us a twilight
before it melted into rain.
But we know it's still there,
whenever a piece of joy falls as crystals
on the cracks and crevices of the floor.

TIME WE LIVE

We live in a time where life matters
as long as we know how to die.
Time was—
as it is now.
Only our dialogues have changed.
Only the way we see faces has taken different forms.
Like the hand that separates a grain from the chaff,
death strips us of all the longings
which we have stored inside our dying brains.

We live in a time where every passing gaze is a
valediction.
And every joining palm yearns
for the days that were left behind.
In this journey of time,
Life shows the river inside a blooming lotus and,
Death brings the other side of life to us.

THE MOON SONG

There are days when
even the moon looks silent in the sky.
There are days when
even a single door bell waits for a finger.
Remember that whenever you buy
three penny worth of time from the dying days,
a hunger is born.

Our fight had always been with ourselves—
in loneliness and in fear.
There we frame our own stories of grief
to feed our distant memories,
to know that we are alive.

Days never remain the same forever.
One dies. While the other grows from it.
As the moon shifts its journey from one corridor to the other,
we perceive our birth from one land to the other
like the resurrection of a bird at each dawn.

WHEN TOMORROW COMES

When tomorrow comes
bring a few oleanders for me.
I will knit them around all the morning stars
and grow a small garden near the sea.
As days are few in numbers,
and nights are longer,
as the only glory of sun lies
when the darkness deepens,
we become what we are meant to be.

My window faces the sea—
to that corner where the moon shines
and leaves its shadow behind.
It showed me light inside
the passing wave of the falling sands.

It was in a different era
when my mother brought me here,
tied my hair with dandelions
and wove stories with her sleepless nights.
I saw her and believed magic to be real.
It was in her that all moments of fear
transformed into delightful ragas
and all sorrows into a rainbow.

If tomorrow comes,
let me wait for the blue evening to rise.

THE NAMELESS

For many years,
I carried a sea in my folds.
The dance of moon and her reverie
have blown it to the island of forgetfulness.

When hope lights dream from summer rain,
we see the landscape of sunset
rising like the coloured fever of a rainbow.

We have created many illusions from the dust of days,
trying to cross our hunger
like riders to the sea.

Seasons come with the turn of clouds.
Lights grow older with every surging wave
when the sun sails down like a burning boat.

SUNLIGHT ON THE HILLS

If you can stop the night
from hanging down the balcony
it will grow into a story of you and me.

Some stories have no beginning,
like that of a pied piper coming down the hill
with a bag of clouds.
His bag carried more dreams
than a night could hold.

When you planted hopes with your solitary hands,
night was smooth like the sound of a bell
ringing through the melting time.

How many years have slipped
from the time when beginning was a story?
A little night with hundred daffodils
is all you need to recreate
a sunlight on the hills.

Purple

Summer is purple here.
Soil carries the scent of wind on dry leaves.
Man here lives on broken glasses, and
grows trees on ashes.

This is the land of desires.
This is the land, where summer brings
magnificence of light from the burning pyre
and winter—
moments of truth in lies,
where love smells of cold, stale food, and
selfishness is a ritual of the bones.

My life grows in this summer,
in this burning pyre.
But often my mind escapes into another,
where man has no faces of man, and
where colour of life is the sky.

Lost in Thunder

Forgetting the yellow clouds,
the mad woman walks over the rims of river
collecting pebbles lost in dreams.
She has feet of ceramic and hands of golden wax
that removes dust from the sea weed.

Forgetting is a misery.
It takes life from its cramped shell
to the hollowness of time's eternal expanse.

Like the beauty that bites dawn in the morning,
there is a balcony hanging down the moon,
falling over our beds each night
when we create cobwebs on the walls.

The madwoman looks through the dark windows of sea
and digs up granites of solitude
from the fingers of sands.

Blood and Dreams

I have given up dreams
to make seasons from my blood.
They will rise up from my body
like lost souls on the Ganges,
and walk on the streets with beggars
lighting a fire on their walls.

Shades of neon in all the moments of twilight
capturing lights of other days.
When sea gives up her solitude to the corals,
madness is reduced to hunger,
and sea moves to the other side of the coin.

I have given up dreams,
to borrow one hundred light years of life
from your nights.

MASKED

Sometimes, when
little clouds bring a winter
to my night,
I hear—
the raw smell of my existence
under the furrows. Under my soiled feet.
In the movement of insects.

Sky has ripped the cloud of rain
and dew drops—
of petals.

Steamed river of innocence
condensed into ignorance,
where truth never recedes
into a beginning.

The gory truth of a silenced existence.

Still,
the habit of possessing the air.
Still,
the obsession of lying under the Sun
Continues… Until…

LIGHT SINKS LOW

Light sinks low as a meandering river,
into the threshold of my windows
when I bake half-grown weeds.
My nails are black with smoke.
I clean the air around me
with my overgrown hair.

My kitchen sink is on the other side
of the green balcony.
It tells me the story of a dead end lane,
winding down the path of trees
like the retreating song of the seagulls.

Here is the place,
where I meet with the falling stars.
Their passion is that of a red sun,
curious for the night to dissolve
into the magnitude of slumberous madness.

I am inhabiting this land
since the beginning of the last century,
collecting feathers from the flying birds
like a jigsaw puzzle.

Inside the blue noon
a boat ferrying rivers,
crosses the horizon.

FRAGMENTS

May flowers fell and
the rain vanished to a distant land of fountains.

We have grown enough of barren lands
from our lost selves
like a hunger is built in each day.
The silence we speak
is louder than the voice of wind.

In the midst of constellation,
I have found you,
at that moment when time was you.

Beginning always has a different story to tell.
We are the children of dead ends
where martyrs kiss the feet of the earth
that once betrayed them.

May flowers were never born.
They are like us,
scripting their own fates
from all the wasted eras given to them
at the hour of anonymity.

SMELLS LIKE SEA

Staying alive is difficult.
You knock the door of your heart,
a lost light flickers in that darkness
like the trembling shadow of a wilting flower.

What does difficult mean to you?
Does it mean you cannot breathe?
Or do you not remember that you are alive?

Memories are like tainted glasses.
You used them with negligence
when you had all the moments in your hand.

Bring me a handful of sand,
and I will show how to build and erase like a sea.

INTO THE VOID

From the shores of night,
some owls and spiders have managed to crawl
from the dense space that humanity had sought for itself.

I hear what the fire inside the comet says
about the fallen grains of summer.
What incapacity to hold on!

For years sunsets have cast
shadows on our bald heads,
like the mysterious lanes of Istanbul,
to create anecdote of memories.

For years I have seen them
coming out of the deprived land
and building fortresses of islands.
I have seen them all...

Love in the time of tragedies
holds more pain than an ocean.

River and the Mahogany

At the far end
where the ticking of clock rides
through the alleyways of fingers,
the square-shaped rusty evenings
manage to erect tombs of despair.

Thousand steps follow me
when I walk in the woods.

A river rises from the leaves
and disappears somewhere…

Was it you calling me through dried up leaves,
when I was searching for a name?

I believe sun will cross the sky
when we'll learn to sing again.
Again there will be fairies in our garden
to compose our lost stories.
Before all the moments fade
we'll build a home of a river and mahogany.

Voices of Shadows

The river wears my shadow,
and under her ripples carries
the grey motion of my heart.
Thousand nights that I lived,
I have seen the dreams of darkness
flowing through the sea of sky,
weaving the story of a girl
who carries a basket of red oleanders.

She speaks the language of the stars
and her silver hair is as blue as mine.
In her eyes grows a river with all its solitude.

I still hear the voices that called my name
at the dusk of winter evenings,
when the sun was sweeter than orange
and all the kites in the sky
dropped like the petals of night.

STILL WATER

There is a place for us—
a place to make garlands of light
from fireflies that burn their wings in the sun;
a place where wind brings the scent of green
and sun pours down rain.

In all the hours of drenched thoughts
when the sun trickles down,
a window to look beyond the sky opens up,
and we see—
the moon with her scythe,
cutting down the dreams of clouds into halves.

There is a place for you and me.
A place to make rivers from dew drops,
a place to colour the wind with water.

Like dropping of light in the ocean,
we have found a place for us.

NECTAR OF ASHES

Some paths lead to the road,
where falling twilight meets
the broken door of the day.

Some paths lead to the dancing woods—
where we dream of butterflies
plucking nectar from our sleep.

Some paths lead to the marigolds and magnolias
where the gardener lifts the dawn from her hair,
and I become the night.

DOWN THE LANE

Summer has its woes.
It has a land which grows in its mind…
incessant as the river of May.
Like the falling of loose sheets of grey
from the ceilings of memories,
summer rests in absurd sorrows.

It crafts stories of our lives.
Whenever music of fireflies
loses itself in the womb of silence,
summer finds its place to live.
Whenever a hundred solitary reapers
cast their shadows on the walls of our lives,
summer moves to the corridor of spring.

AUTUMNAL VISIONS

In autumn sky
you can see a horse riding on the dolphin's ear
and a mustard flower,
evaporating like the smoke of a seed.
Like the fruitless flower of a lotus,
earth takes its shape.

Some of our stories of grief
look like the closed doors.
Some of our sweat, smell like sun-dried fields.
In autumn,
dance of girls change as the cloud of winter,
and in its green sky we can hear rustling of leaves
like the beating of drums.

DREAMS TO FLY

Let the windows up;
so that we can see our lost souls
unwinding to the other side of the road.

We have been separated
since last rain on the hills
like two magnolias
that have blown with the wind.

Several solitary sunsets have brought
numerous lingering shadows on our paths
which meet with a thousand stars.

Our destinies have carved their own stories
on the waves of time.
And where the rain finds its wings,
we find our dreams to fly.

THE TWO ROADS

Roads are two.
One that leads you to the alleyways of dreams,
and other to the land of distant memories.
They are inseparable like the two wings of a dove
flying to and fro,
in and out of our sleep.

Roads are two.
To a man who harvests under full moon,
the roads bring two silver coins to measure his toil,
to show him life in half-lived lives of the trees.
Their ends are many—
like hundred winds on the corn fields
blowing into the disheveled feet of a farmer.

I stand on the brink of time,
where my fingers try to hold
all the inessential infinities,
as a mad man tries to touch the stars
over his sun burned head.
Their ends have brought me here,
to the last leaf of the sea
where dreams and memories would cross.

COLOURS

Your hands are like the fingers of morning,
cold as the stones flowing under a river
and blue like a night.
You move within the four walls of my body
to measure light and darkness of this earth, and
to count the rise and fall of sands.

You sing with a voice that knows
the colours of the dusks and blue midnight sun.
And many of those hours when the green sea
sobs like a woman to become herself.

Red sky is your wings
that lie over the dawns and my green breasts.
You die with all these,
with the cold fever of my body, and
a thousand other nights around you.

HEART OF A RAINBOW

In the heart of a rainbow
where the mist carries the morning in its palm,
grows a landscape of Blue Mountains and marigolds.
Eyes of the streets do not lie
like the hands of a clock.
They move through corridors of wind
and walls elude them.

In the heart of a rainbow,
all the swans that once carried me
in their blue eyes to my mother,
are lost now like the butterflies of rain.

LINES WRITTEN IN SEPTEMBER

Few lines I will write.
Few lines on this wind on my face
erasing past lines of a broken shadow.
Few lines on this summer afternoon
when the clouds immersed in rain
lash against the pane of my September heart.

I am stuck amidst the graveyard of memories
playing with a few numbers,
playing with the wind.
And in this hour of madness
when you sing to my lips,
what a joy it is to get drenched in the rain!

STREETS OF FORGETFULNESS

Streets of forgetfulness are forever grey.
Grey in different shades and forms.
When the twilight breaks and diffuses,
and the sky gathers mist,
my mind that plays with all its encounters
gathers slowly all the solitary days' turbulent ends
in reason and in madness.

But in madness alone
streets frame colours around the mid-day sun
in solitude and despair.
The invisible light that it uses to cover itself
encircles my mind
when I count the numberless seasons in my hands,
and wait for the approaching hour.

AT DUSK

When dusk falls
heart feels like a journey in solitude—
cold as the air inside a sea-shell,
beautiful as the voice of a storm.

It frees chains,
brings impenetrable lights from darkness
which gives mirror to madness of mind
and the madness,
a soul.

The dusk falls,
and world melts like the ringing of bells in a temple,
distant as the paths of a river
and invisible like sparrows of dawn.

DREAM WALK

It is like a dream when
we walk over the phosphorous lands and silicone rivers,
and fingers of road bleed the tune of a broken song;
when nights pour water of marbles
and my shoulders grow fins.

Everything else seems green.
It is only in dream that things are purple
and as pure as solitude, where
a rose garden and lake of yellow rubies grow and die,
and the other half of ourselves
create memories of night.

PURE AS SORROWS

Some sorrows rising like the suns of soil,
are those that borrow laughter
from the joys of butterflies,
to know where the graves of tomorrow lie.

Sorrows are like the children of summer.
They know from where the wind of life blows,
and where the sun borrows its light.

The dark horses of sun,
ride over the shores of night
to paint the blue dawn with feathers of sorrow.

Sorrows are like those—
born from the silver heart of the earth,
and rise towards the fire
where a life is born each day from the golden wings of sun.

WORDS FALL LIKE PAINTINGS

Your white face named me black.
Words from your eyes fall like paintings
from yellow twilight of the sky.
And these words have colours in them.
My colour is black as the mourning sun,
dark as the thought that floats at midnight.
It is like the petals of a blue rose
and I saw it growing out of my navel,
like trees on the Burmese mountains.

But your face, the white you carry in your skin
grows like petals without the rose.
And when you sleep, I see the stars of my face
blinking through the lips and pores of your eyes.

NIGHTS OF RED LILIES

Nights of red lilies,
your petals bloom through the soft murmur of sorrows
like the rose-coloured bells of dawn.
I hold you in my palms and leave you
among the ruined hearts. Among the forbidden fruits of life.

Your sorrows are like the shape of a boat,
that sail through your white hair
like a lost bird on the sea.
You never know the count of coins that fall on us.

Nights of red lilies,
you are the dream,
that death desired.

ONE WHO HAS LOST HIS SOUL

In the whirlwind of your madness
my life grows.
Your tongue brings words from the fires
and burns my soul that sleeps
with earthworms and citrus leaves.

Your madness is like the dance of wind
in a forest and,
like the one who carries a rainbow in his wallet.

I had the heart of a silver noon
where I carried your sighs of autumn.
A heart without life.

Now I wear that silver around my arms,
and empty my heart to receive
the wild silence of your madness
where my life will rise.

ROOTS

The roots of the night
have the black salt of my heart,
sprouting through the veins of my nails.

I have a desire—
to break open the silence of the streets
and see the burning incense of thunder.

There is music in all these,
like that of a broken glass on the table.
I sprinkle the dust of my sweat
to make the thunder more musical.

BEYOND YOUR EYES

Whenever I tried to look beyond your eyes,
the goose with its golden wings
moves over the spaces of geometrical light,
and scatters feathers over the drunken grasses.

Nights of useless dreams
have shaped the trees like stars.

Through the looking glass
your painless sorrow looks like a swan.
And your eyes—
like a mirror
that moon holds to the earth,
whenever I tried to look beyond your eyes.

WHEN THE WIND BROKE INTO A SONG

When the wind broke into a song,
my voice grew old like the clay feet of the day.
It grew old not because the time wasn't same
as it used to be in those evenings
when I returned home with a few jasmines.
It is old because the sun has forgotten to rain.

Like forests that come in dreams,
the wind with its song comes and goes.
But I wanted to hold it in my hand
and play it till the day's end.

Music has long evaded me
since the time my hair was green,
and eyes saw rainbow dreams.
It is now all about the sound of silence,
growing louder day by day like movement of grasses
on a windy day.

I do not call it despair,
as it is the wind
that borrowed the light from me
to break itself into a song.

LOST WORDS

I do not speak for rain.
I speak for those wings which bring the sky
from the forefinger of mountains
to the ocean's blue eyes.
Like the clock that stops at noon,
I swing and hang in the air with all the salts of sweat
and try to understand what fireflies in the bush
say about the burden of glowing.

I do not speak for rain.
I speak for those trees that grow from their ashes
and show pains of humanity in the veins of a leaf.
I speak for those butterflies that are born
out of those hours that brought east to the west,
and showed us life inside a sleeping grain.

I do not speak for rain,
but it is now all the rains
that I have in my hand to bring back the lost words.

TREES HAVE WINGS

Tress give birth at night
from womb of ashes that the sea brings
in its madness to the earth.
I sleep with those roots around my neck
and rise with the deep voice of wind.

The girl who walks barefoot on sand,
knows not how much a handful of sand cost.
I do not know how many heaps of sand
we create each day to forget the memories.
But I know that the day
which brings sea to the shore,
is another dream where we sing, dream,
and make love with the nights.

WHEN ALL IS LOST

Strange is the night,
that lets winter descend the stairs of alleys
with raw bricks and stones.
The tremulous minds find an escape
to move across the lines,
to rise above the feet of day,
to know where waves meet the sea.

Hands of clay make stones of hunger
to write over the sunbeams—
a desolate thunder of words.

I have lost the syllables of Time.
I have lost my days
where pain meets pain,
to join with the cracks of sand,
where the sea builds its home.

Now when all is lost,
I have filled my hands with the gifts of losses
to create another night,
where winter will ascend the stairs of my shoulders
and give me rains to fly.

THE LAST ROSE

Have you seen a dying rose turning into a deer
foraging for a pasture into the forest?
If you have eyes that can build fortresses of clay,
from the remains of sea shells
like the sun that forms stars from its heart,
then each day a deer would be born of a rose.

Things are not what we see always.
There are layers of what we see and what we do not.
Pure vision is like a drop of dew on the petal,
rising like clouds on a hill top.
Our eyes have gone too weary from seeing
what we are not meant to see.

Like midnight's dream that ends with a sigh,
the rose dies,
and another story of a deer is born from her.

SOME THINGS NEVER END

In this land of darkness,
the only light that shines is the one
you plucked for me from the fading dreams
of the sunflowers that were blooming in your eyes,
when I waited for rain.
As a star loses its way in the night,
I have found the lost delusion of time
from the heaps of forgotten journeys.

Mind is a strange box of allegory
lined with entangled boughs of indistinct nightmares.
We are mere dream walkers in it,
searching for a meaning lost in wilderness
like a woman in delirium.

In this land of darkness,
the only light that shines is the one
you showed me when I failed to write,
a few couplets for the rain.

PLACE BEYOND

If there was a place beyond all the doors,
and the unknown roads,
then all that is said and done would fall back
to the space from where it once began.

Everybody here is in love.
Except us.
Everyone knows where a bird meets the horizon.
But for us it is the night's shadows that arrest
the motion of our hearts.

We live inside a cemetery nowadays—
with red mosses and algae around us.
Here, dark clouds fall with the rain
and evaporate in our fingers.
We do nothing,
but count the number of roses that are born
and die each day.

Death cannot cross these lines and reach us.